GOD IS

BOBBY C GRAHAM

MOTTO

God is a Spirit: and they that worship him must worship him in spirit and in truth.

FOREWORD

I Greet you in Jesus most Holy name

It's a honor to be marry to this great man who written this book (God Is) I am grateful

For taking part in it I Dr. Sandra Graham can also relate to this anointed topic God Is been marry to Dr B C Graham I get the chance to witness the ups and downs seeing him going through difficult situations and believe me I understand who God Is. My precious brothers and sisters I want to encourage you to realize that there is nothing that God cannot bring us through be cause God Is the beginning and the end, the first and the last, Alpha and Omega he is a rewarder of those who deligent seek him he is a lawyer in the court room a judge on the judgement seat a doctor in a sick room a heart fixer a heart regulator.

A peace maker and to sum it out God is who he say he is he is everything and going through different things I truly understand when he told Moses to say I am that I am.

Bishop Johnny Lloyd

Dear BC Graham School of Ministry Family,

I greet you in the grace and peace of our Lord Jesus Christ. I write to you today to share my continues to inspire and drive me each day.

I firmly believe that our ministry is founded on a divine calling to shepherd God's people. Jesus as Jesus, the Good Shepherd, left no one behind, I am dedicated to guiding and nurturing every member of our community. I see our work as a journey of transformation-where Gods unmerited grace meets every heart in need, offering healing, restoration, and hope.

At the core of my ministry is the conviction that God's grace has power to change lives. I have witnessed, time and again, how His unconditional love and forgiveness can break chains and ignite hope, even in the darkest circumstances. This transformative power inspires me to create spaces where each person can encounter the life changing reality of Jesus Christ.

Our pursuit of peace, gratitude, and love is not only a personal mission but also a collective one. I am passionate about the empowering you to live out your God-given purpose. Whether through teaching, mentoring, or everyday acts of kindness, I believe that each of us can be a beacon of Gods love and an instrument of His peace in our world.

I also embrace the challenges of our time as opportunities to learn further into God's promises. I trust that every setback is a setup for a greater breakthrough, and I encourage you to do the same. Together, we are co-laborers in building a future where God's light shines brightly in every corner of life.

Thank you for your dedication, your prayers, and your willingness to be part of this journey. As we continue to serve, learn, and grow, may we always remember that our work is not merely a role- it is a calling from God, and the best is yet to come

In His service and with heartfelt gratitude.

John 13:34-35

A new commandment I give unto you. That ye love one another, as I have loved you, that ye also love one another. By this shall all men know that ye are my disciples, that ye have love one for another.

Giving Honor to God Almighty and His Son Jesus the Christ. Founders Bishop and 1st Lady Graham, Brother and Sisters. Shalom. From the moment Bishop Graham obeyed the voice of God and saw the ministry that God had placed me. Furthermore confirmed the love that His daughter and I shared has really been a blessing to tremendous blessing to

my life. BBCGTS has allowed me to become spiritually, mentally and emotionally mature, equipping me with the necessary tools to be a soldier for the Lord. Bishop Graham is not only my founder but He's my Spiritual Leader and through his leadership and guidance, he has set the foundation, for past alumnus, present students, and future prospects to be great ambassadors for Christ. Words from our founder, "Everything moving by the power! God bless.

Bishop Antwon McNeil

Greetings brothers and sisters I am Dr Irvin West I bring you great joy the man name Dr B C Graham is a true leader whom I admire and I know for certain if you are looking for someone who treat everyone the same he is the one and Dr Graham favorite word is Everything moving by the power of God

Humble summited

Dr Irvine West

From the desk of the Administrator

Dr Sharon West

To Godbe the Glory I like back and wonder how the Lord brought me over over 53 years ago I grew up in school with the Founder Dr B C Graham what a blessing to be in fellowship with a very dear friend and now he is my Pastor my heart was running over when he chose me to have the position of Administrator I truly know he is a man of God and I summits my heart and time to do my best in pleasing our Lord and Savior so friends if you are looking for a trueful leader DR Graham is a great leader

yours in Christ

Dr Sharon West

I am Dr. Cheristerlyn Brooks a native of Statesboro Georgia and a proud

Alumni of BC Graham Theological Seminary.

BC Graham Theological Seminary means so much to me and my ministry.

It was at BC Graham Theological Seminary I found my purpose and my love. I

had a mandate from God to raise I up end time warriors to advance the

Kingdom of God and BC Graham Theological Seminary provided me the way

to do it. Through BC Graham Theological Seminary the Training for Reigning

Bible Institute was birth and has now been fulfilling the mandate.

I have been graced to serve along side Dr. BC Graham to help him fulfill his mandate to open schools across this country to advance the Kingdom of God. Through my leadership BC Graham is the banner school for Dominion Bible Institute located in Ghana West Africa in Takarodi, Elubo and Kasoa making BC Graham Theological Seminary International. I serve as the ambassador for the school and travel back and to representing BC Graham Theological Seminary. I am grateful to be able to be a source of strength, encouragement and balance by God's grace to this second to none school.

Greetings in the name of our Lord and Savior Jesus Christ. God has allowed me to accomplish many goals in my life, but one of the greatest goals that I have accomplished was attending the BC Graham Theological Seminary. The BC Graham Theological Seminary has been such a blessing to me. One of the many blessings was receiving my Doctorate Degree in Theology. The next greatest blessing was becoming the Dean of the state of Florida for the BC Graham Theological Seminary. I am so grateful and so proud of the founder Dr. Bobby Charles Graham. A man of God that not only works with you but he stands beside you every step of the way. My desire is to see many achieve their dreams and aspirations through this seminary.

Sincerely

Dr Tonda Wells D.DIV.

Dean of the State of Florida

In perilous times like these it's imperative that we hear from God. Nevertheless there are so many people that have given up on their source to getting God's information which is the truth. Bobby

Graham Ministries has been a very strong vocal point for ministering the truth. If there was ever anyone that not hesitant about spreading the gospel as the truth there is none other than Bobby Graham himself. Hats off to this ministry God will continue to bless you withstanding the world you have displayed an attitude of not compromising to the world regardless of what appears to be popular. You will be rewarded God bless you keep the faith and continue to press toward the mark at the end of this journey I'll look over faithful and say to you, job well done my faithful Brother God brought us here just like he promised.

Attorney Reginald Sessions

(Second Page)

Psalms 27

The Lord is my light and salvation, whom shall I fear? The Lord is the strength of my life; of whom shall I be afraid?

First giving honor to God who is the head of my life, to my husband Bishop Antwon McNeil Sr., to my father and mother Bishop and First Lady Elect Bishop Graham and to everyone in their respective places.

As First Lady, Elder, and In-Coming President of this Elite Seminary, this has been a journey. God has really been good to me, through the good, the bad and the ugly, God has remained faithful. I have learned to trust in God with my whole heart and to lean not to my own understanding. I have experienced that, through faith, all things are possible. Bishop Graham founder, and my earthly father has really guided me through this process and his guidance has taught me significance of faith. That faith is the key to Gods heart and that faith is one of the key components of becoming a prominent leader. With that being said, it really gives me great pleasure to be appointed your future President.

With Great Regards,

Elder/First Lady

Mrs. Jessica McNeil

TESTIMONIAL.

John 13:34-35 A new commandment I give unto you. That ye love one another, as I have loved you, that ye also love one another. By this shall all men know that ye are my disciples, that ye have love one for another.

Giving Honor to God Almighty and His Son Jesus the Christ. Founders Bishop and 1st Lady Graham, Brother and Sisters. Shalom. From the moment Bishop Graham obeyed the voice of God and saw the ministry that God had placed me. Furthermore confirmed the love that His daughter and I shared has really been a blessing to tremendous blessing to

my life. BBCGTS has allowed me to become spiritually, mentally and emotionally mature, equipping me with the necessary tools to be a soldier for the Lord.Bishop Graham is not only my founder but He's my Spiritual Leader and through his leadership and guidance, he has set the foundation, for past alumnus, present students, and future prospects to be great ambassadors for Christ. Words from our founder, "All things moving by the power! God bless.

Bishop Antwon McNeil

Being a part of BC Graham Theology Seminary Bible College is a source of great pride in my life. I embrace the excitement that comes from being deeply invested in our shared purpose and actively pursuing the goal of teaching God's word. The opportunities presented here challenge me to expand my skills, broaden my knowledge, and step boldly outside my comfort zone. I also cultivate powerful bonds with individuals who share my passions and life experiences, fostering a sense of belonging for all we encounter. As the Director of Education, I dedicate my time and talents to uplifting others and contributing to meaningful social causes, leaving a positive mark on the world.

Dawn King

GOD IS

As I sit on this Saturday night reflecting deep in my mind about who God Is, then I truly understand why I'm writing this book and amed it "God Is". Truly God Is who He says He is. He is a rewarder of those who seek him. I can remember as though it was yesterday when the doctor said in 1999 that I wouldn't live to see the next day. Boy, doesn't time fly! To my understanding its 2023. It's nothing that Bobby has done, but its "God Is" who He says he is. I see so many people that look over who God really is. Just let me name a few; He is a doctor when we are sick, a lawyer to defend us when we are in trouble, a bridge over troubled waters, a mind regulator, a heart fixer, a mother when we are motherless, a father when we are fatherless, a brother and sister, a friend when we need a friend. I mean just naming a few, God Is something I can say day in and day out and still never get through saying it. I see people talk God with their mouth, but their heart stands a distance from their mouth. Yes, this is the day and time that men and women, boys and girls should call on God because He is who He says He is!

I travel from coast to coast and I see so many things. But God Is speaking to us through so many forms, my question is, are we listening? When I started preaching 49 years ago, I didn't understand Matthew 24, Luke 21 and Mark 13. Yes, we see wars and rumors of wars, famines, earthquakes, nations against nation., Yes, my friends, the Bible or maybe I should say the Word of God Is being fulfilled.

Sickness and diseases are filling up the hospitals and nursing homes. Death is filling up the funeral homes and the churches are being thinned out. But, according to the word of God that day should not come except there come a falling away. Men are falling from grace every day. Sometimes it seems like there are more churches than people, but I know that God Is doing whatever it takes to get us on our knees and pray. Just pause for a moment and look at

II Chronicles 7, you may ask yourself a question and say who God Is to you? One may say one thing and another say another thing, the facts are God can and will do what He says He will do.

When my mind was troubled with the weight of the world God gave me a piece of mind. Even David sang and praised himself out of whatever situation he was in and we can do the same thing. (I Peter 5:7)

I once heard the Lord say he would never leave or forsake us. He has proven that so many times to me. In this day and hour I find myself praying like never before. Yes, I know Jesus is coming back but mainly I want to be right when he comes back. God please help us in this hour of pain.

Psalm 51

Have mercy upon me, O God, according to thy lovingkindness: according unto the multitude of thy tender mercies blot, out my transgressions.

Wash me thoroughly from mine iniquity, and cleanse me from my sin.

For I acknowledge my transgressions: and my sins ever before me

Against thee, thee only, have I sinned, and done this evil in thy sight: that thou mightiest be justified when thou speakest, and be clear when thou judgest.

Behold, I was shapen in iniquity; and in sin did my mother conceive me.

Behold, thou desirest truth in the inward parts; and in the hidden part thou shalt make me to know wisdom.

Purge me with hyssop, and I shall be clean: wash me, and I shall be whiter than snow.

Make me to hear joy and gladness; that the bones which thou hast broken may rejoice.

Hide thy face from my sins, and blot out all mine iniquities.

Create in me a clean heart, O God; and renew a right spirit within me. Cast me not away from thy presence; and take not thy holy spirit from me.

Restore unto me the joy of thy salvation; and uphold me with thy free spirit.

Then will I teach transgressors thy ways; and sinners shall be converted unto thee.

Deliver me from blood guiltiness, O God, thou God of my salvation: and my tongue shall sing aloud of thy righteousness.

O Lord, open thou my lips; and my mouth shall shew forth thy praise.

For thou desirest not sacrifice; else would I give it: thou delightest not in burnt offering.

The sacrifices of God are a broken spirit: a broken and contrite heart, O God, thou wilt not despise.

Do good in thy good pleasure unto Zion: build thou the walls of Jerusalem.

Then shalt thou be pleased with the sacrifices of righteousness, with burnt offering and whole burnt offering: then shall they offer bullocks upon thine altar.

I've travelled all over through the Seminary, trying to educate God's people through Biblical knowledge, some except, some refuse. I look at it like Jesus said; one plant, one water, God gives the increase. Sometimes we as a people miss out on what God Is trying to tell us because we are weighted down with the cares of the world and God Is not of the things of the world. It's about Heaven. So, we must let go of things that is holding us back.

Hebrews 12

Wherefore seeing we also are compassed about with so great a cloud of witnesses, let us lay aside every weight, and the sin which doth so easily beset us, and let us run with patience the race that is set before us,

Looking unto Jesus the author and finisher of our faith; who for the joy that was set before him endured the cross, despising the shame, and is set down at the right hand of the throne of God.

For consider him that endured such contradiction of sinners against himself, lest ye be wearied and faint in your minds.

Ye have not yet resisted unto blood, striving against sin.

And ye have forgotten the exhortation which speaketh unto you as unto children, My son, despise not thou the chastening of the Lord, nor faint when thou art rebuked of him:

For whom the Lord loveth he chasteneth, and scourgeth every son whom he receiveth.

If ye endure chastening, God dealeth with you as with sons; for what son is he whom the father chasteneth not?

But if ye be without chastisement, whereof all are partakers, then are ye bastards, and not sons.

Furthermore we have had fathers of our flesh which corrected us, and we gave them reverence: shall we not much rather be in subjection unto the Father of spirits, and live?

For they verily for a few days chastened us after their own pleasures; but he for our profit, that we might be partakers of his holiness.

Now no chastening for the present seemeth to be joyous, but grievous: nevertheless afterwards it yieldeth the peaceable fruit of righteousness unto them which are exercised thereby.

Wherefore lift up the hands which hang down, and the feeble knees;

And make straight paths for your feet, lest that which is lame be turned out of the way; but let it rather be healed.

Follow peace with all men, and holiness, without which no man shall see the Lord:

Looking diligently lest any man fail of the grace of God; lest any root of bitterness springing up trouble you, and thereby many be defiled;

Lest there be any fornicator, or profane person, as Esau, who for one morsel of meat sold his birthright.

For ye know how that afterward, when he would have inherited the blessing, he was rejected: for he found no place of repentance, though he sought it carefully with tears.

For ye are not come unto the mount that might be touched, and that burned with fire, nor unto blackness, and darkness, and tempest,

And the sound of a trumpet, and the voice of words; which voice they that heard intreated that the word should no be spoken to them anymore:

(For they could not endure that which was commanded, And, if so much as a beast touch the mountain, it shall be stoned or thrust through with a dart:

And so terrible was the sight, that Moses said. I exceedingly fear and quake:)

But ye are come unto mount Sion, and unto the city of the living God, the heavenly Jerusalem, and to an innumerable company of angels,

To the general assembly and church of the firstborn, which are written in heaven, and God the Judge of all, and to the spirits of just men made perfect,

And to Jesus the mediator of the new covenant, and to the blood of sprinkling, that speaketh better things than that of Abel.

See that ye refuse not him that speaketh. For if they escaped not who refused him that spake on earth, much more shall not we escape, if we turn away from him that speaketh from heaven:

Whose voice then shook the earth: but now he hath promised, saying, Yet once more I shake not the earth only, but also heaven.

And this word, Yet once more, signifieth the removing of those things that are shaken, as of things that are made, that those things which cannot be shaken may remain.

Wherefore we receiving a kingdom which cannot be moved, let us have grace, whereby we may serve God acceptably with reverence and godly fear:

For our God Is a consuming fire.

I John: 2:

My little children, these things write I unto you, that ye sin not. And if any man sin, we have an advocate with the Father, Jesus Christ the righteous:

And he is the propitiation for our sins: and not for ours only, but also for the sins of the whole world.

To Know God Is to Obey

And thereby we do know that we know him, if we keep his commandments.

He that saith, I know him, and keepeth not his commandments, is a liar, and the truth is not in him

But whoso keepeth his word, in him verily is the love of God perfected: hereby know we that we are in him.

He that saith he abideth in him ought himself also so to walk, even as he walked.

Brethren, I write no new commandment unto you, but an old commandment which ye had from the beginning. The old commandment is the word which ye have heard from the beginning.

Again, a new commandment I write unto you, which thing is true in him and in you:

 because the darkness is past, and the true light now shineth.

He that saith he is in the light, and hateth his brother, is in darkness even until now.

He that loveth his brother abideth in the light, and there is no occasion of stumbling in him.

But he that hateth his brother is in darkness, and walketh in darkness, and knoweth not whither he goeth, because that darkness hath blinded his eyes.

I write unto you, little children, because your sins are forgiven you for his name's sake.

I write unto you, fathers, because ye have known him that is from the beginning. I write unto you, young men, because ye have overcome the wicked one. I write unto you, little children, because ye have known the Father.

I have written unto you, fathers, because ye have known him that is from the beginning. I have written unto you, young men, because ye are strong, and the word of God abideth in you, and ye have overcome the wicked one

Love not the world, neither the things that are in the world. If any man love the world, the love of the Father is not in him.

For all that is in the world, the lust of the flesh, and the lust of the eyes, and the pride of life, is not of the Father, but is of the world.

And the world passeth away, and the lust thereof: but he that doeth the will of God abideth for ever.

Beware of Seducers

Little children, it is the last time: and as ye have heard that the antichrist shall come, even now are there many antichrists; whereby we know that it is the last time.

They went out from us, but they were not of us; for if they had been of us, they would no doubt have continued with us: but they went out, that they might be made manifest that they were not all us.

Live in Christ

But ye have an unction from the Holy One, and ye know all things.

I have not written unto you because ye know not the truth, but because ye know it, and that no lie is of the truth.

Who is a liar but he that denieth that Jesus is the Christ? He is the antichrist that denieth the Father and the Son.

Whosoever denieth the Son, the same hath not the Father: but he that acknowledgeth the Son hath the Father also.

Let that therefore abide in you, which ye have heard from the beginning. If that which ye have heard from the beginning shall remain in you, ye also shall continue in the Son and in the Father.

And this is the promise that he hath promised us, even eternal life.

These things have I written unto you concerning them that seduce you.

But the anointing which ye have received of him abideth in you, and ye need not that any man teach you: but as the same anointing teacheth you of all things, and is truth, and is no lie, and even as it hath taught you, ye shall abide in him.

And now, little children, abide in him; that when he shall appear, we may have confidence, and not be ashamed before him at his coming.

If ye know that he is righteous, ye know that everyone that doeth righteousness is born of him.

Just reflecting back on when Jesus went up to the mountain to pray and fast, he was tempted from Satan offering him things of the world. But because he had the Word in him, used the power of the Word to rebuke Satan with his worldly gifts. We must understand that the gifts of the world are temporary, but the gift of God is eternal. David described it best in...

Psalm 121

I will lift up mine eyes unto the hills, from whence cometh my help.

My help cometh from the Lord, which made heaven and earth.

He will not suffer thy foot to be moved: he that keepeth thee will not slumber.

Behold, he that keepeth Israel shall neither slumber or sleep.

The Lord is thy keeper: the Lord is thy shade upon thy right hand.

The sun shall not smite thee by day, nor the moon by night.

The Lord shall preserve thee from all evil: he shall preserve thy soul.

The Lord shall preserve thy going out and thy coming in from this time forth, and even for evermore.

The things on earth are eye catching to take our minds off of heaven. Paul once quoted from the Old Testament… "eyes hath not seen, nor ears heard what God has prepared for those who love him." One of the greatest singers of all times sung a song, "I Love the Lord." Why don't you take time to ask yourself a question, do you love the Lord? Jesus told his disciples; If you love me feed my Sheep, meaning people; when Jesus started this journey, he told men if you put down your fishing net; I will make you fishers of men. Indeed, there is people out there that need to be hooked with the Word of God. On earth we fish for breams, catfish, bass, red snapper, trout and so on. My Brothers and Sisters, let's fish for drugs, drug users, drug abusers, crack heads, prostitutes, thieves, murders, liars, wicked people soon and let's bring them to Christ, not looking at what they are doing, but looking at what they can do. Remembering the word of God… "If any man be in Christ he is a new creature. The former things are passed away and behold all things are new." Yes indeed, just to think about the old Bobby Charles Graham brings tears to my eyes. But yet and still I am grateful because He could have taken me, but He is the God of another chance. "God Is!"

He told his angels go down there and lead Bobby Charles Graham unto the path of righteousness for His name sake. I had a whole lot of problems. But I can lift up my hands and say, "Lord, I thank you for allowing me to see a brand new day!" Yes, David said it and I believe it. This is the day that the Lord hath made. Let us rejoice and be glad in it. I sit here in the house of the Lord surrendering praises unto the Almighty saying what a mighty God we serve.

At the age of 65 I couldn't be any happier! Yes, I have trials and tribulations, but I also have a God who stands by me through it all. I realize that the most powerful thing we can do is pray.

Jesus told us that man should always pray and not to faint. I once heard a song "Jesus, Jesus, Jesus, Savior, Savior, Savior!" Lord, I need you because I know without you, I am nothing. I am calling on you like never before. I heard in your Word, let the Redeem of the Lord say so.

As I travel throughout this country I see hills, mountains, oceans, rivers, land, animals, trees, people, buildings houses, machines; all I can say is God Is. Man thinks that he is doing it all. But how, unless it's a God somewhere. Let's take time to look at Psalms 24 in its entirety.

Psalm 24

David Calls All to Worship

The earth is the Lord's, and the fulness thereof; the world, and they that dwell therein.

For he had founded it upon the seas, and established it upon the floods.

Who shall ascend into the hill of the Lord? or who shall stand in his holy place?

He that hath clean hands, and a pure heart; who hath not lifted up his soul unto vanity, nor sworn deceitfully.

He shall receive the blessing from the Lord and righteousness from the God of his salvation.

This is the generation of them that seek him, that seek thy face, O Jacob Selah.

Lift up your hands, O ye gates; and be ye lift up, ye everlasting doors; and the King of glory shall come in.

Who is the King of glory? The Lord strong and mighty, the Lord mighty in battle.

Lift up your heads, O ye gates; even lift them up, ye everlasting doors; and the King of glory shall come in.

Who is this king of glory? The Lord of hosts, he is the King of glory. Selah.

In my early years I heard the song "Father I Stretch my Hands to Thee." There is no other help I know. And yes, I have a charge to keep and it's only because God Is. I remember 44 years ago when God sent an angel into the hospital in Fort Gaines, GA and took my daughter. She was in a room where other babies were and God allowed his angel to take her and leave the other babies. With that being said God Is. Yes! Yes! Yes! God Is. He is too wise to make a mistake! I have been through life's journey and it amazes me to see God operate in the greatness of His power. Yes, there is black power, white power, money power, drug power, relationship power! But there is no power like the Power of God! Please take a moment and help me say, "God Is!"

God is so powerful until He can calm down the raging sea. Even when we get caught up in ourselves, he knows how to calm us down. Brothers and Sisters, we are no match with God!

I once heard an old saying, "if you can't beat them join them." So, what I have learned is to join them, because it's safe too. I smile when I say this, because of the last book I wrote, "That God of Ours," can fix what has been broken, release what's been bound, open what's been closed, close what's been open, dry what's been wet and wet what's been dry! Please say it with me, "God Is."

In 2008 I wrote a book called "We Are On A Journey". Think about it! I know in life sometimes it gets hard, but knowing who God Is will bring you through. I know I have had my share of troubles. God's grace and mercy brought me through. I realize who God Is and the Power of His Resurrection. Truly, it was God's grace and mercy that brought me through.

Let's take a little time and Pray;

"Dear Jesus I am thankful for the opportunity to tell you how grateful I am that you took time out of your busy schedule to dispatch your angels to let them know to wake up your humble servant and give him an assignment to fulfill the work of a devoted minister, to teach your people the Word of God. To let them know that the time is drawing near and to blow the trumpet to let your people know that time is almost here".

Lord when I see the miracles that you are performing, it makes me sit back and say, "God Is" and you are my everything. I bless your name now more than ever. Lord your people need your help. It's so good to say your people have your word, but Jesus they need to live your Word.

Down here in Ft. Pierce Florida during the hour that the sun begins to go down, sitting here on the beach realizing who God really is, thinking about when Jesus was walking on the water and the disciples was so amazed until Peter asked could he do it as well. Jesus for who he was the Son of God, told Peter to come and Peter did so until he got afraid then he began to sink and Jesus reached out his hand to save him. What I am saying is our destiny determines according to our Faith. Talk nor sight doesn't move God, Faith moves God.

Hebrews 11:

Now faith is the substance of things hoped for, the evidence of things not seen.

For by it the elders obtained a good report.

Through faith we understand that the worlds were framed by the word of God, so that things which are seen were not made of things which do appear.

By faith Abel offered unto God a more excellent sacrifice than Cain, by which he obtained witness that he was righteous, God testifying of his gifts: and by it he being dead yet speaketh.

By faith Enoch was translated that he should not see death; and was not found, because God had translated him: for before his translation he had this testimony, that he please God.

But Without faith it is impossible to please him: for he that cometh to God must believe that he is, and that he is a rewarder of them that diligently seek him.

By faith Noah, being warned of God of things not seen as yet, moved with fear; prepared an ark to the saving of his house; by the which he condemned the world, and became heir of the righteousness which is by faith.

By faith Abraham, when he was called to go out into a place which he should after receive for an inheritance, obeyed; and he went out, not knowing whither he went.

By faith he sojourned in the land of promise, as in a strange country, dwelling in tabernacles with Isaac and Jacob, the heirs with him of the same promise:

For he looked for a city which hath foundations, whose builder and maker is God.

Through faith also Sara herself received strength to conceive seed, and was delivered of a child when she was past age, because she judged him faithful who had promised.

Therefore sprang there even of one, and him as good as dead, so many as the stars of the sky in multitude, and as the sand which is by the sea shore innumerable.

These all died in faith, not having received the promises, but having seen them afar off, and were persuaded of them, and embraced them, and confessed that they were strangers and pilgrims on the earth.

For they that say such things declare plainly that they seek a country.

And truly, if they had been mindful of that country from whence they came out, they might have had opportunity to have returned.

But now they desire a better country, that is, an heavenly: wherefore God is not ashamed to be called their God: for he hath prepared for them a city.

By faith Abraham, when he was tried, offered up Isaac: and he that had received the promises offered up his only begotten son,

Of Whom it was said, That in Isaac shall thy seed be called:

Accounting that God was able to raise him up, even from the dead; from whence also he received him in a figure.

By faith Isaac blessed Jacob and Esau concerning things to come.

By faith Jacob, when he was a dying, blessed both the sons of Joseph; and worshipped, leaning upon the top of his staff.

By faith Joseph, when he died, made mention of the departing of the children of Israel;

And gave commandment concerning his bones.

By faith Moses, when he was born, was hid three months of his parents, because they saw he was a proper child; and they were not afraid of the king's commandment.

By faith, Moses when he was come to years, refused to be called the son of Pharoah's daughter;

Choosing rather to suffer affliction with the people of God, than to enjoy the pleasures of sin for a season;

Esteeming the reproach of Christ greater riches than the treasures in Egypt: for he had respect unto the recompence of the reward.

By faith he forsook Egypt, not fearing the wrath of the king; for he endured, as seeing him wo is invisible.

Though faith he kept the Passover, and the sprinkling of blood, lest he that destroyed the firstborn should touch them.

By faith they passed through the Red Sea by dry land: which the Egyptians assaying to do were drowned.

By faith the walls of Jericho fell down, after they were compassed about seven days.

By faith the harlot Rahab perished not with them that believed not, when she had received the spies with peace.

And what shall I more say? for the time would fail me to tell of Gedeon, and of Barak and of Samson, and of Jephthae; of David also, and Samuel, and of the prophets:

Who through faith subdued kingdoms, wrought righteousness, obtained promises, stopped the mouths of lions,

Quenched the violence of fire, escaped the edge of the sword, out of weakness were made strong, waxed valiant in fight, turned to flight the armies of the aliens.

Women received their dead raised to life again: and others were tortured, not accepting deliverance; that they might obtain a better resurrection:

And others had trial of cruel mockings and scourings, yea, moreover of bonds and imprisonment:

They were stoned, they were sawn asunder, were tempted, were slain with the sword: they wandered about in sheepskins and goatskins; be destitute, afflicted, tormented;

(Of whom the world was not worthy:) they wandered in deserts, and in mountains, and in dens and caves of the earth.

And these all, having obtained a good report through faith, received not the promise:

God having provided some better thing for us, that they without us should not be made perfect.

Ephesians 3:1-21

For this cause I Paul, the prisoner of Jesus Christ for you Gentiles,

If ye have heard of the dispensation of the grace of God which is given me to you-ward:

How that by revelation he made known unto me the mystery; (as I wrote afore in few words,

Whereby, when ye read, ye may understand my knowledge in the mystery of Christ)

Which in other ages was not made known unto the sons of men, as it is now revealed unto his holy apostles and prophets by spirit;

That the Gentiles should fellow heirs, and of the same body, and partakers of his promise in Christ by the gospel:

Whereof I was made a minister, according to the gift of the grace of God given unto me by the effectual working of his power.

Unto me, who am less than the least of all saints, is this grace given, that I should preach among the Gentiles of the unsearchable riches of Christ;

And to make all men see what is the fellowship of the mystery, which from the beginning of the world hath been hid in God, who created all things by Jesus Christ;

To the intent that now unto the principalities and powers in heavenly places might be known by the church the manifold wisdom of God,

According to the eternal purpose which he purposed in Christ Jesus our Lord:

In whom we have boldness and access with confidence by the faith of him.

Wherefore I desire that ye faint not at my tribulations for you, which your glory.

For this cause I bow my knees unto the Father of our Lord Jesus Christ,

Of whom the whole family in heaven and earth is named,

That he would grant you, according to the riches of his glory, to be strengthened with might by his Spirit in the inner man;

That Christ may dwell in your hearts by faith; that ye, being rooted and grounded in love,

May be able to comprehend with all saints what is the breadth and length, and depth, and height;

And to know the love of Christ, which passeth knowledge, that ye might be filled with all the fulness of God.

Now unto him that is able to do exceeding abundantly above all that we ask or think, according to the power that worketh in us,

Unto him be glory in the church by Christ Jesus throughout all ages, world without end. Amen.

Luke 1:37

For with God nothing shall be impossible.

When I was a boy, I didn't understand when they said, "In His hand He held the world." Now looking at the things that God has in control, I can truly say what a Mighty God we serve.

Look at what God allows man to make; boats, ships, cars, bridges for cars to cross.

I see one doing this and another doing that i.e., people fishing, swimming, having picnics, playing music. All I can say is, God Is.

My mind went back in the old days when God confound the language of the people. I see one doing this and another doing that, all I can say is God Is. Laying here on a towel, watching the birds flying, air planes flying, borders of water and condos alongside the beach.

I remember Jesus once telling a man with one talent how he had buried it in the earth, he hid his Lord's treasure. I remember myself how that I let the pressure of life bound me. I was so bound as though I had forgot my writing, it was hid from me, somewhere in bondage, my writing was buried from me; until one day I was standing on the outside of the house in Arlington, my spiritual father drove by and saw me. He stopped and asked me to go help him on 612 Appletree Street. His name was Dr. James Brown, Sr. After going there to help the owner of the house where we were working. The owner's name was Sandra Carpenter. After meeting her, we began to reflect on the Word of God and little did I know my gift for writing came back after thirteen years of being hidden.

Today I know that Sandra was that Angel God placed in my life, my mind goes back to when Paul met Timothy after learning that his mother and grandmother raised him up right. All Paul did was stir up the gift that was in him. Lois and Eunice were their names.

God uses whomever He will. I will forever be grateful for Sandra who came into my life.

Again, I say God Is what we need. The Democrats say we need a Democrat, the Republicans say we need a Republican, but no matter who you choose whether Democrat or Republican, God is still in control. As a man of God, I think we need to go back to the basics when men put God first in everything. I remember when God told David even if he made his bed in hell he was there. Even though man have forgotten about who God Is, he is still God.

We live on a planet that everything gets man's attention but God. We can hardly get children to read or carry a Bible, but playing loud music. Boys and men walking around with their pants hanging off their waist, saying words that are not decent and children playing in the streets. God doesn't have any pleasure in the ways of some of these young people and believe me if we don't reach out and gain God in our lives we are going to go down like the floor. We must have joy and peace in our hearts. Solomon prayed to God for the people in II Chronicles Chapter 7 and in Romans Chapter 10.

Please Brothers and Sisters let's join hands and bow our heads before God's Grace and seek his face, for the needs of the nation (worldwide); regardless of race, creed or color that you may be.

We need to come together as one in Christ Jesus our Lord and Savior, no matter what kingdom we are serving. We pray that God's kingdom be done on earth as it is in Heaven.

Let's stop seeking the creation and start seeking the Creator because the creation is only the things of the world, it all belongs to God. Start seeking the Creator and his rightness and see that God will do what he said he would do. Again I say, God will do what he says he will do. Remember when Solomon prayed for wisdom and knowledge so that he could led God's people? He prayed for wisdom from God not from man. God made Solomon become the wise man in the world and he did not only make him the wise man, but he also made him the richest.

Even the Queen of Sheba came to see the wisdom of Solomon. What I am saying is, let's go back to the basics. God is the same today as he was then. All we have to do is trust him.

St. John 3:16. Romans 5:23.

Remember God made man in His image. Solomon did not pray for things to make him big, but he prayed for the people because we were made in God's image. Jesus told his disciples to love the brethren as I have loved you.

Deuteronomy 6:

Instead of asking God for anything, we have to start thanking God for what he has already given us. When we seek God first the things we need will come. Man looks at your outward appearance, God looks at the heart. Just please check this out, "Trust In The Lord!"

After talking to Sandra, while writing this book, she told me about things concerning seeking God first. Knowing that she needed electric, plumbing, and different things done to her house, God didn't just send her a plumber, He sent her a man that could do everything that the house needed and also sent her a Soul Mate. Only God could have sent her someone who could understand and had patience with her. After understanding who God Is by listening to her testimony, it showed who this God Is.

WHO GOD IS

Scripture References

John 4:24

God is spirit, and those who worship him must worship in spirit and truth.

John 4:8

For (His disciples had gone away into the city to buy meat.)

John 14:6

Jesus said to him, I am the way, the truth, and the life, No one comes to the Father except by Me.

Revelation 22:13

I am the Alpha and the Omega, the Beginning and the End, the First and the Last.

1 John 4:16

And we have known and believed the love that God has for us, God is love, and he who abides in love abides in God, and God in him.

Exodus 3:14

And God said unto Moses, I AM THAT I AM: and he said, Thus shalt thou say unto the children of Israel   I AM hath sent me unto you.

Numbers: 23:19

God is not man, that he should lie; Nor the son of man, that he should repent: Hath he said, and shall he do it? or has he spoken, and shall he not make it good?

Titus 1:2

In hope of eternal life, which God, who cannot lie, promised before the ages began.

Luke 18:27

And he said, The things which are impossible with men are possible with God.

Colossians 1:16

For by him all things were created, that are in heaven and that are on earth, visible and invisible, whether they be thrones, or dominions or principalities or powers: all things were created through him, and for Him.

Deuteronomy 7:9

Know therefore LORD your God, he is God, the faithful God, which keepeth covenant and mercy with them that love him and keep his commandments to a thousand generations;

Genesis 1:1

In the beginning God created the heavens and the earth.

I John 3:1-24

Behold, what manner of love the Father has bestowed upon us, that we should be called sons of God" therefore the world knoweth us not, because it knew him not.

Beloved, now we are the sons of God; and it has doth not yet appear what we shall be: but we know that, when he shall appear, we shall be like him; for we shall see him as he is.

And Every man that hath this hope in him purifieth himself, even as he is pure.

Whosoever committeth sin transgresseth also the law; for sin is the transgression of the law.

And ye know that he was manifested to take away our sins; and in him is no sin. Whosoever abideth in him sinneth not; whosoever sinneth hath not seen him, neither known him.

Little children, let no man deceive you: he that doeth righteousness is righteous, even as he is righteous.

He that committeth sin is of the devil; for the devil sinneth from the beginning. For this purpose the Son of God was manifested, that he might destroy the works of the devil. Whosoever is born of God doth not commit sin; for is seed remaineth in him: and he cannot sin, because he is born of God.

In this the children of God are manifest, and the children of the devil: whosoever doeth not righteousness is not of God, neither he that loveth not his brother.

For this is the message that ye heard from the beginning, that we should love one another.

Not as Cain, who was of that wicked one, and slew his brother. And wherefore slew he him? Because his own works were evil, and his brothers righteous.

Marvel not, my brethren, if the world hate you.

We know that we have passed from death unto life, because we love the brethren. He that loveth not this brother abideth in death.

Whosoever hateth his brother is a murderer: and ye know that no murderer hath eternal life abiding in him.

Hereby perceive we the love of God, because he laid down his life for us: and we

Ought to lay down our lives for the brethren

But whoso hath this world's good, and seeth his brother have need, and shutteth up his bowels of compassion from him, how dwelleth the love of God in him?

My little children, let us not love in word, neither in tongue; but in deed and in truth.

And hereby we know that we are of the truth, and shall assure our hearts before him.

For if our hearts condemn us, God is greater than our hearts, and knoweth all things.

Beloved, if our hearts condemn us not, then have we confidence toward God.

And whatsoever we ask, we receive of him, because we keep is commandments, and do those things that are pleasing in his sight.

And this is his commandment, That we should believe on the name of his Son Jesus Christ, and love another, as he gave us commandment.

And he that keepeth his commandments dewelleth in him and he in him. And thereby we know that he abideth in us, abideth in the Spirit which he hath given us.

Romans 5:8

But God demonstrates his love toward us, in that, while we were yet sinners, Christ died for us.

1 Timothy 1:17

Now to the King eternal, immortal, invisible, the only wise God, be honour and glory for ever and ever.

John 1:1

In the beginning was the Word, and Word was with God, and the Word was God.

Isaiah 41-10

Fear thou not; for I am with thee: be not dismayed; for I am thy God: I will strengthen thee; yea, I will help thee; yea, I will uphold thee with the right hand of my righteousness.

John 3:16

For God so loved the world, that he gave his only begotten Son, that whoever believes in Him should not perish, but have everlasting life.

John 1:14

And the Word became flesh, and dwelt among us, (and we beheld His glory, the glory as of the only begotten of the Father,) full of grace and truth.

Deuteronomy 4:31

(For the Lord thy God is a merciful God;) he will not forsake thee, neither destroy thee, nor forget the covenant of thy fathers which he sware unto them.

John 8:24

I said therefore unto you, that ye shall die in your sins: for if ye believe not that I am he, ye shall die in your sins.

Zephaniah 3:17
The Lord thy God in the midst of thee is mighty; he will save, he will rejoice over thee with joy; he will rest in his love, he will joy over thee with singing.

Philippian's 4:13
I can do all things through Christ which strengtheneth me.

Hebrews 4:12
For the word of God is quick, and powerful, and sharper than any twoedged sword, piercing even to the dividing asunder of soul and spirit, and of the joints and marrow, and is a discerner of the thoughts and intents of the heart.

John 12:45

And he that seeth me, seeth him that sent me.

Exodus 34:6-7

And the Lord passed by before him, and proclaimed, The Lord, The Lord God, merciful and gracious, longsuffering, and abundant in goodness and truth,

Keeping mercy for thousands, forgiving iniquity and transgression and sin, and that will by no means clear the guilty; visiting the iniquity of the fathers upon the children, and upon the children's children, unto the third and to the fourth generation.

Colossians 2:9

For in him dwell all the fulness of the Godhead bodily.

Psalm 34:3

O magnify the Lord with me, and let us exalt his name together.

John 3:16-17

For God so loved the world, that he gave his only begotten Son, that whosoever believeth in him should not perish, but have everlasting life.

For God sent not his Son into the world to condemn the world; but that the world through him might be save.

James 1:17

Every good gift and every perfect gift is from above, and comes down from the Father of lights, with whom is no variation, neither shadow of turning.

1 John 5:9-10

If we receive the witness of men, the witness of God is greater: for this is the witness of God which he hath testified of his Son.

He that believeth on the Son of God hath the witness in himself: he that believeth not God hath made him a liar; because he believeth not the record that God gave of his Son.

Galatians 3:28

There is neither Jew nor Greek, there is neither bond nor free, there is neither male nor female: for ye are all one in Christ Jesus.

Psalm 27:1

The Lord is my light and my salvation; whom shall I fear? The Lord is the strength of my life; of whom shall I be afraid?

Isaiah 44:6

Thus saith the Lord the King of Israel, and his redeemer the Lord of hosts; I am the first, and I am the last; and beside me there is no God.

Psalm 86:5

For thou, Lord, art good, and ready to forgive; and plenteous in mercy unto all them that call upon thee.

Joshua 1:9

And afterward the children of Judah went down to fight against the Canaanites, that dwelt in the mountain, and in the south, and in the valley.

1 John 1:5

This then is the message which we have heard of him, and declare unto you, that God is light, and in him is no darkness at all.

Hebrews 1:3

Who being the brightness of his glory and the express image of his person; and upholding all things by the word of his power, when he had by Himself purged our sins, sat down at the right hand of the Majesty on high;

Romans 6:23

For the wage of sin is death; but the gift of God is eternal life through Jesus Christ our Lord.

1 Chronicles 16:11

Seek the Lord and his strength, seek his face continually.

Revelation 1:1

The Revelation of Jesus Christ, which God gave unto him, to shew unto his servants things which must shortly come to pass; and he sent and signified it by his angel unto his servant John:

John 17:3

And this is life eternal, that they might know thee the only true God, and Jesus Christ, whom thou hast sent.

II Samuel 7:22

Wherefore thou art great, O Lord God: for there is none like thee, neither is there any God beside thee, according to all that we have heard with our ears.

Isaiah 40:28

Hast thou not known? hast thou not heard, that the everlasting God, the Lord, the Creator of the ends of the earth, fainteth not, neither is weary? There is not searching of his understanding.

Psalm 83:18

That men may know that thou, whose name alone is JEHOVAH, art the most high over all the earth.

Ephesians 2:3-6

Among whom also we all had our conversation in times past in the lusts of our flesh, fulfilling the desires of the flesh and of the mind; and were by nature the children of wrath, even as others.

But God, who is rich in mercy, for his great love where with he loved us,

Even when we were dead in sins, hath quickened us together with Christ, (by grace ye are saved;)

I Corinthians 10:13

There hath no temptation taken you but such as is common to man: but God is faithful, who will not suffer you to be tempted above that ye are able; but will with the temptation also make a way to escape, that ye may be able to bear it.

II Timothy 1:7

For God hath not given us the spirit of fear; but of power, and of love, and of a sound mind.

Psalm 23:1-6

The Lord is my shepherd; I shall not want.

He maketh me to lie down in green pastures: he leadeth me beside the still waters.

He restoreth my soul: he leadeth me in the paths of righteousness for his name's sake.

Yea, though I walk through the valley of the shadow of death, I will fear no evil: for thou art with me; thy rod and thy staff they comfort me.

Thou preparest a table before me in the presence of mine enemies: thou anointest my head with oil; my cup runneth over.

Surely goodness and mercy shall follow me all the days of my life: and I will dwell in the house of the Lord for ever.

Psalm 11:7

For the righteous Lord loveth righteousness; his countenance doth behold the upright.

1 John 1:9

If we confess our sins, he is faithful and just to forgive us our sins, and to cleanse us from all unrighteousness.

Psalm 145:9

The Lord is good to all: and his tender mercies are over all his works.

Malachi 3:6

For I am the Lord, I change not; therefore ye sons of Jacob are not consumed

Isaiah 57:15

For thus saith the high and lofty One that inhabited eternity, whose name is Holy; I dwell in the high and holy place, with him also that is of a contrite and humble spirit, to revive the spirit of the humble, and to revive the heart of the contrite ones.

Isaiah 40:28-29

Hast thou not known? hast thou not heard, that the everlasting God, the Lord, the Creator of ends of the earth, fainteth not, neither is weary? There is no searching of his understanding.

He giveth power to the faint; and to them that have no might he increaseth strength.

Revelation 1:8

I am Alpha and Omega, the beginning and the ending, saith the Lord, which is to come, the Almighty.

Deuteronomy 33:27

Th eternal god is thy refuge, and underneath are the everlasting arms: and he shall thrust out the enemy from before thee; and shall say, Destroy them.

Roman 8:28

And we know that all things work together for good to them that love God, to them who are the called according to his purpose.

II Corinthians 5:21

For he hath made him to be sin for us, who knew no sin; that we might be made the righteousness of God in him.

Deuteronomy 6:4

Hear, O Israel: The Lord our God is one Lord:

Mark 10:18

And Jesus said unto him, Why callest thou me good? there is none good but one, that is, God.

Isaiah 55:8-9

For my thoughts are not your thoughts, neither are your ways my ways, saith the Lord.

For as the heavens are higher than the earth, so are my ways higher than your ways, and my thoughts than your thoughts.

Isaiah 9:6

For unto us a child is born, unto us a son is given: and the government shall be upon his shoulder: and his name shall be called Wonderful, Counselor, The mighty God, The everlasting Father, The Prince of Peace.

Psalm 86:15

But thou, O Lord, art a God full of compassion, and gracious, longsuffering, and plenteous in mercy and truth.

John 20:28

And Thomas answered and said unto him, My Lord and my God.

Psalm 119:68

Thou art good, and doest good; teach me thy statutes.

II Timothy 3:16-17

All scripture is given by inspiration of God, and is profitable for doctrine, for reproof, for correction, for instruction in righteousness:

That the man of God may be perfect, throughly furnished unto all good works.

Psalm 106:1

Praise ye the Lord. O give thanks unto the Lord; for he is good: for his mercy endureth for ever.

Deuteronomy 4:35

Unto thee it was shewed, that thou mightiest know that the Lord he is God; there is none else beside him.

Isaiah 46:9

Remember the former things of old: for I am God, and there is none else; I am God, and there is none like me.

Isaiah 44:24

Thus saith the Lord, thy redeemer, and he that formed thee from the womb, I am the Lord that maketh all things; that stretcheth forth the heavens alone; that spreadeth abroad the earth by myself;

Matthew 28:19

Go ye therefore, and teach all nations, baptizing them in the name of the Father, and of the Son, and of the Holy Ghost:

Psalm 50:10-12

For every beast of the forest is mine, and the cattle upon a thousand hills.

I know all the fowls of the mountains: and the wild beasts of the field are mine.

If I were hungry, I would not tell thee: for the world is mine, and the fulness thereof.

John 10:30-33

I and my Father are one.

Then the Jews took up stones again to stone him.

Jesus answered them, Many good works have I shewed you from my Father; for which of those works do ye stone me?

Naham 1:7

The Lord is good, a strong hold in the day of trouble; and he knoweth them that trust in him.

Psalm 23:1

The Lord is my shepherd; I shall not want.

1 Corinthians 1:9

God is faithful, by whom ye were called unto the fellowship of his Son Jesus Christ our Lord.

John 8:58

Jesus said unto them, Verily, verily, I say unto you, Before Abraham was, I am.

1 Chronicles 16:34

O give thanks unto the Lord; for he is good; for his mercy endureth for ever.

Matthew 19:26

But Jesus beheld them, and said unto them, With men this is impossible; but with God all things are possible.

James 2:19

Thou believest that there is one God; thou doest well: the devils also believe, and tremble.

II Corinthians 13:14

The grace of the Lord Jesus Christ, and the love of God, and the communion of the Holy Ghost, be with you all. Amen

Psalm 18:30

As for God, his way is perfect: the word of the Lord is tried: he is a buckler to all those that trust in him.

Genesis 18:14

Is anything too hard for the Lord? At the time appointed, I will return unto thee, according to the time of life and Sarah shall have a son.

1 Peter 5:6-7

Humble yourselves therefore under the mighty hand of God, that he may exalt you in due time:

Casting all your care upon him; for he careth for you

Galatians 5:22

But the fruit of the Spirit is love, joy, peace, longsuffering, gentleness, goodness, faith,

Proverbs 3:19

The Lord by wisdom hath founded the earth; by understanding hath he established the heavens

Psalm 136:1

O give thanks unto the Lord; for he is good: for his mercy endureth for ever.

Ephesians 4:6

One God and Father of all, who is above all, and through all, and in you all.

Revelation 1:17-18

And when I saw him, I fell at his feet as dead. And he laid his right hand upon me, saying unto me, Fear not; I am the first and the last:

I am he that liveth, and was dead; and, behold, I am alive for evermore, Amen; and have the keys of hell and of death.

1 Timothy 4:4

For every creature of God is good, and nothing to be refused, if it be received with thanksgiving:

James 1:20

For the wrath of man worketh not the righteousness of God.

1 Timothy 2:5

For there is one God, and one mediator between God and men, the man Christ Jesus;

Matthew 28:18

And Jesus came and spake unto them, saying, All power is given unto me in heaven and in earth.

Psalm 18:31

For who is God save the Lord? or who is a rock save our God?

John 5:18

Therefore the Jews sought the more to kill him, because he not only had broken the sabbath, but said also that God was his Father, making himself equal with God.

Jeremiah 29:11

For I know the thoughts that I think toward you, saith the Lord, thoughts of peace, and of evil, to give you an expected end.

THE NEW SERENITY PRAYER

By: Fr. James Marin, SJ

God, grant me the serenity to accept the people I

cannot change, which is pretty much everyone

since I'm clearly not you, God.

At least not the last time I checked

And while you're at it, God, please give me the

Courage to change what I need to change about

myself, which is frankly a lot, since, once again

I'm not you, which means I'm not perfect

It's better for me to focus on changing myself

than to worry about changing other people,

who, as you'll no doubt remember me saying,

I can't change anyway.

Finally, give me the wisdom to just shut up

whenever I think that I'm clearly smarter

than everyone else in the room,

that no one knows what they're talking about

except me, or that I alone have all the answers.

Basically, God grant me the wisdom to

remember that I'm not you.

Graham Chapel Deliverance and Peace Ministries INC.

Bishop Bobby C Graham Theological Seminary

5358 13th Street

Malone, FL 36345

Testimonies

(This page should be by itself)

www.ingramcontent.com/pod-product-compliance
Lightning Source LLC
LaVergne TN
LVHW061602070526
838199LV00077B/7148